ACT LIKE MEN

THE BIBLE STUDY

JAMES MACDONALD
WITH NEIL WILSON

LifeWay Press® Nashville, Tennessee

Published by LifeWay Press® • © 2017 James MacDonald
Reprinted September 2018

No part of this book may be reproduced or transmitted in any form or by any means, electronic or mechanical, including photocopying and recording, or by any information storage or retrieval system, except as may be expressly permitted in writing by the publisher. Requests for permission should be addressed in writing to LifeWay Press®; One LifeWay Plaza; Nashville, TN 37234.

ISBN 978-1-4627-9617-5 • Item 005802240

Dewey decimal classification: 248.842
Subject headings: MEN / CHRISTIAN LIFE / BIBLE.
N.T. 1 CORINTHIANS 16—STUDY AND TEACHING

Unless indicated otherwise, all Scripture quotations are from the ESV® Bible (The Holy Bible, English Standard Version®), copyright © 2001 by Crossway, a publishing ministry of Good News Publishers. Used by permission. All rights reserved. Scripture quotations marked NKJV are taken from the New King James Version®. Copyright © 1982 by Thomas Nelson. Used by permission. All rights reserved. Scripture quotations marked KJV are taken from the Holy Bible, King James Version. Scripture quotations taken from the New American Standard Bible® (NASB), Copyright © 1960, 1962, 1963, 1968, 1971, 1972, 1973, 1975, 1977, 1995 by The Lockman Foundation. Used by permission. www.lockman.org. Scripture quotations marked NIV are taken from the Holy Bible, New International Version®, NIV®. Copyright © 1973, 1978, 1984, 2011 by Biblica Inc.™ Used by permission of Zondervan. All rights reserved worldwide. www.zondervan.com. The "NIV" and "New International Version" are trademarks registered in the United States Patent and Trademark Office by Biblica Inc.™

To order additional copies of this resource, write to LifeWay Resources Customer Service; One LifeWay Plaza; Nashville, TN 37234; fax 615-251-5933; call toll free 800-458-2772; email orderentry@lifeway.com; order online at LifeWay.com; or visit the LifeWay Christian Store serving you.

Printed in the United States of America

Groups Ministry Publishing • LifeWay Resources
One LifeWay Plaza • Nashville, TN 37234

CONTENTS

2 Timothy 1:7 God did not give us a spirit of timidity, but a spirit of power, of love, and of self discipline.

ABOUT THE AUTHOR

JAMES MACDONALD (D. Min. Phoenix Seminary) has committed his life to the unapologetic proclamation of God's Word. He is the founder and Senior Pastor of Harvest Bible Chapel which began in 1988 with eighteen people and now welcomes thirteen thousand people to its seven Chicago-area campuses each week.

His practical Bible teaching is heard daily around the world on radio and TV through the program *Walk in the Word*, and more than one hundred and seventy churches have been planted on four continents under Dr. MacDonald's leadership. He continues to recruit, train, and equip pastors to plant Vertical Churches through Mission Harvest and the Vertical Church Pastor Training Center.

James's extensive ministry also includes the worship and songwriting ministry Vertical Worship, the film-making ministry Vertical Church Films, the accredited Pre-K through grade twelve Harvest Christian Academy, a year-round camp, and a center for biblical counseling.

James has authored several books and Bible studies, including: *Act Like Men*; *Vertical Church*; *Lord, Change Me*; *Lord, Change My Attitude*; *When Life is Hard*; *Always True*; and most recently, *The Will of God IS the Word of God*.

James and Kathy are thrilled to be close to their seven grandchildren and three adult children, who serve alongside them in ministry.

FIND OUT MORE ABOUT JAMES AND HIS MINISTRIES AT:

WalkintheWord.org
HarvestBibleChapel.org
VerticalOfficial.com
HarvestChristianAcademy.org
VerticalChurchFilms.org

Instagram: @pastorjamesmacdonald
Twitter: @jamesmacdonald
Facebook: /DrJamesMacDonald
Podcast (audio): James MacDonald—
Walk in the Word
Podcast (video): James MacDonald—
Walk in the Word TV

WELCOME TO *ACT LIKE MEN*

I'll keep this short, because after years of hanging out with men, preaching to men, and even longer being a man myself, I realize that brevity gets to a man's heart and mind sometimes even faster than the food route. Act Like Men isn't theoretical; it's practical. It's doing it, making mistakes, learning lessons, and continuing to act like men even, and especially, when we are overwhelmed by how far we still have to go to get it right.

I've called this a field manual because the words workbook, guide, and even journal didn't quite get the job done. Field manual implies you're at it. You're engaged and committed. The decision to act like a man has already been made, and you are paying attention to what is required every day. You are no longer parked by the road (or stuck in the ditch), but you're in the traffic of daily life, looking for the signs that will keep you on the narrow path.

If you're tracking with me, you will be amazed that after decades of studying Scripture, I was shocked the first time I read two verses tucked into the last chapter of 1 Corinthians. They waited there a long time to hit my life like four thunder booms and a bolt of lightning. Memorize these verses because they will recalibrate your thinking and give you a jolt of truth every time you wonder what God expects from you as a man.

> *Be watchful,*
> *stand firm in the faith,*
> *act like men,*
> *be strong.*
> *Let all that you do be done in love.*
> **1 CORINTHIANS 16:13-14**

As you engage with this field manual on your own and with other men, I'm praying you will let these five phrases become the description of your life, not perfectly, but increasingly. God not only expects you to act like a man; He is powerfully eager to help you do it (Phil. 1:6).

So, act like men.

GETTING THE MOST FROM YOUR *ACT LIKE MEN* FIELD MANUAL

When it comes to acting like men, there's a major "on-your-own" part and a major "with-other-guys" part of the plan. Guys that fail to act like men have often tried to go it alone. Over and over again in the Bible when Satan wants to do serious damage, he goes after a man alone. So, a band of brothers is crucial. But sometimes guys have failed to act like men because they are spending too much time with other men who have no interest in acting like men. This field manual offers you help for when you're going it alone and when you're with other committed men.

GROUP SESSIONS

Make it a priority to be there. Don't miss the opportunity to work together with other guys on this challenge to act like men. Bring your questions to the sessions, and discover how other guys are dealing with the same issues you are. Do the follow-through exercises and come ready to share what you are discovering.

THE BIBLE

The instruction and directives found in *Act like Men* didn't come out of a focus group, and they aren't the result of creative musings on my part. They are from God, recorded in Scripture. Each of the five phrases from 1 Corinthians 16:13-14 summarizes an entire range of actions or skills that the rest of God's Word can clarify for you. Keep your Bible open and close by during these studies. God can and will guide you through His Word.

FOLLOW-THROUGH

I like to golf. Playing golf reminds me a lot of the process of acting like men. Every time I address the ball, regardless of where I landed from my previous shot, is a new test of attention and technique. No shot is automatic. You can never phone in a swing. And one of the critical, often overlooked aspects of every shot is the follow-through. A great-looking swing downward can go terribly wrong in the follow-through. This could vividly explain why the ball went somewhere radically different than the target.

The follow-through principle applies to many sports, but it applies most critically to life. The three follow-through exercises after each group session are designed to help you reflect on and act on what you learn in the group time. They are intended to guide you as you internalize and apply each of the phrases in 1 Corinthians 16:13-14. Don't skip the follow-throughs.

At the end of each set of follow-through exercises, you will find a notation about parallel content in the book *Act Like Men*.

ACT LIKE MEN BOOK

A valuable companion, *Act Like Men* is a book by the same title published by Moody Publishers. It contains a forty-day series of devotionals created to help you think through the various aspects of acting like men. I realized a long time ago that I couldn't expect men to be honest about themselves and their inner struggles unless I was willing to be honest about mine. Writing that book reminded me over and over again of how far God has brought me, but it also confronted me with how far I still have to go. By God's grace through faith I am a saved man, still working out my salvation with fear and trembling, as I trust Him in all things to help me increasingly act like His man. I trust you will rise to that same challenge.

TIPS FOR LEADERS

CHECK OUT A LESSON

Familiarize yourself with the session components:

- **Watch:** Each session begins with a brief teaching video from James MacDonald. We have noted some key statements from each video and listed them as fill-in-the-blank statements on the viewer guides. We've included the answers to the blanks on page 95.

- **Group Discussion:** The video teaching is followed by a time for men to process and discuss what they heard. Several questions and discussion prompts are provided.

- **Follow-through:** There are three follow-through exercises following each session to reinforce what was taught in the teaching videos and group sessions. These are to be completed between the group sessions.

PREVIEW THE VIDEO

Watch the teaching video before each session in order to be able to field questions and lead the discussion more calmly and confidently.

PRAYER

Spend time in prayer as you prepare to lead your group. After you have the names of your group members, pray for each one by name. Find different ways to use prayer in each session, including opening and closing as well as praying for needs that arise. Also provide time for men to pray together in twos or small groups.

PROVIDE RESOURCES

As you prepare for each session, take note of any resources (Bible verses, books, articles) that might help you and the other men in your group understand and apply the truth.

EMPHASIZE ENCOURAGEMENT

Look for opportunities to encourage. Appreciate transparency on the part of group members. Understand how risky it is, and affirm those who are willing to share.

LEAD BY EXAMPLE

Don't ask the group to do anything you haven't already done or aren't willing to do.

FOLLOW UP

Touch base with the guys in your group outside of the group session. Text them with encouragement. Call if you sense they are struggling.

EVALUATE

Take a few minutes to evaluate after each session. Maybe even ask a group member to give his input. Think through the following questions: *What could be done better? How is the group responding? What are some examples of progress?*

WEEK 1

INTRO

COMPLETE THE VIEWER GUIDE BELOW AS YOU WATCH TEACHING SESSION 1.

WHAT IS *ACT LIKE MEN*?

1. It began as a _____.

2. It was a _____ _____.

3. It was a _____.

4. It became a _____.

WHAT DOES *ACT LIKE MEN* MEAN?

1. Don't act like a _____.

2. Don't act like an _____.

3. Don't act like a _____.

4. Don't act like a _____.

DISCUSS

DISCUSS THE VIDEO TEACHING WITH YOUR GROUP.

1. Our culture seems to hold or portray two standards when it comes to men: 1) How men *should* act, and 2) how men *do* act. The first standard can be positive and challenging. The second leans toward being negative and demeaning, especially from what we see in media. What behaviors would you say the culture assigns to each of those two categories?

   • How men *should* act:

   • How men *do* act:

2. What man in your life best exemplifies authentic manhood? What qualities in this man's life prompted you to choose him?

3. If you could go back and explain to a much younger you what it means to act like a man, what would you include in your explanation?

4. In our culture, what rites of passage or moments mark when and how a boy becomes a man? To what degree are those experiences true markers of becoming a man?

5. In what situations are you most likely to find yourself asking, "What would an authentic man do right now?"

6. When and how did you become a man? Do you think there's a role for other men to play in helping someone else reach manhood? Explain.

7. How can the rest of us pray for you this week as we start on this journey to act like men together?

_____

_____

_____

_____

_____

_____

_____

_____

_____

_____

_____

_____

_____

_____

_____

_____

_____

_____

_____

_____

WEEK 1

PERSONAL BIBLE STUDY

Pick up your Bible. If you mainly use a Bible app on your phone, indulge me for a few minutes and get your paper and print Bible. Hold it in your hands. Look closely at it. The Bible is a book and yet so much more, in similar fashion to how a piece of paper is just paper until you realize it's also a love note from your wife. You can treat the Bible as just a book until you realize at gut level that it is filled with stuff God really wants you to know. You may not think you need to know a lot of it, but since it is from God, what you think about its contents doesn't matter— you need to know it.

Find 2 Timothy 3:16-17 in your Bible, and read it out loud to yourself. I could print those verses here, but that would defeat my purpose—to get you to open God's Word. Those two verses tell you how the Bible came to be, four ways it is useful (or profitable), and why it is crucial in learning to act like men. Now take three minutes to write, in the space provided, everything God brings to mind as you meditate on the phrase: "that the man of God may be complete, equipped for every good work."

FOLLOW-THROUGH 1:
A MAN OF GOD

In the group session, we talked about the different views our culture brings to the phrase "act like men." Some expectations are negative ("Men are naturally slobs.") and some are positive. ("Men should take care of their families.") We approach the phrase "act like men" with a particular context in mind. For our discussion, we want to focus on the word *men*. Our phrase actually means, *act like (a certain kind of) men*. This week we want to think about specific traits or qualities that God includes (or excludes) in His expectations for the kind of men we ought to be.

Review the four "don't act like" statements from the teaching video. Which of these statements presents you with the most significant challenge right now? Why? What needs to change?

What not to do is a helpful starting place or turning point, but it doesn't give you a lot of direction. Knowing what not to do or what you have to stop doing begs the question: So what *should* I do? For those answers, we turn to Scripture.

> *¹⁴But as for you, continue in what you have learned and have firmly believed, knowing from whom you learned it ¹⁵and how from child-hood you have been acquainted with the sacred writings, which are able to make you wise for salvation through faith in Christ Jesus. ¹⁶All Scripture is breathed out by God and profitable for teaching, for reproof, for correction, and for training in righteousness, ¹⁷that the man of God may be complete, equipped for every good work.*
> **2 TIMOTHY 3:14-17**

Yes, I know you've already looked at verse 17, but we've got to get this passage nailed down if we're going to be serious about acting like men. I've left the verse numbers in so we can talk about specific verses. This passage is all about what it takes to be a quality man, a man of God.

First, a little background. This passage is part of a letter the apostle Paul wrote to a young man named Timothy. Paul sent Timothy out as his messenger and his representative on the ground. This letter includes many instructions and much encouragement for Timothy and, by extension, for us.

> **In verses 14-15, circle all the words that have to do with understanding and grasping an important concept. (Hint: You should be able to find at least five.) In the space provided, write these two verses in your own words.**

Paul reminded Timothy of the most important and basic truth about being a man of God: "salvation through faith in Christ Jesus" (v. 15). In two weeks, we'll begin to look at how to "stand firm in the faith." But before we can *stay and stand* in the faith, we have to be *in* it. At his core, a man of God is a man who knows he is saved by God through faith in Christ Jesus.

Here's my question to you right now: Are you such a man? Do you know you are saved by God through faith in Christ Jesus? I'm not asking if you have some kind of understanding of how salvation happens. I'm asking if you've experienced it yourself. In another passage, Paul described the necessary response to Christ this way: "'The word is near you, in your mouth and in your heart' (that is, the word of faith that we proclaim); because, if you confess with your mouth that Jesus is Lord and believe in your heart that God raised him from the dead, you will be saved. For with the heart one believes and is justified, and with the mouth one confesses and is saved" (Rom. 10:8-10).

> **In the space provided, briefly describe the moment when you believed in your heart and confessed with your mouth that Jesus is Lord.**

If you have to honestly say, *I've really never done that,* please know that you can do it right now. If you sense God's Spirit calling you to give your life to Christ, don't hesitate. If you're not sure where to start, you can pray the following prayer to express your repentance of sin and faith in Christ: *God, I recognize that I am a sinner, and I can't save myself. I realize that's why Jesus came to die in my place on the cross. I accept His sacrifice on my behalf and confess that He is Lord of my life. I acknowledge that You raised Jesus from the dead and that He lives today and can enter my life by His Spirit right now. I gladly welcome Him. Thank You, Lord, for saving me. In Jesus' name, Amen.*

If you just prayed that prayer of faith and repentance, you need to tell someone—confess with your mouth that Jesus is now your Lord and Savior. Call up someone you know who is a follower of Jesus and simply tell him, "I trusted Christ as my Savior and Lord today." You will make his day!

Back to 2 Timothy 3 for a moment. I know you've already read and thought some about verse 17, but I don't want you to miss the act like men connection in this verse. Once you are a man of God by faith in Christ, it's time to immerse yourself in God's Word so that you can become "complete, equipped for every good work" (2 Tim. 3:17). The word *complete* doesn't mean finished, but rather "in fit shape or condition."[1] Men who act like God's men are continually growing more capable and competent in the truth, being equipped for the work of Christ. If this study has its intended effect on your life, it won't be the finishing touch. Men who act like men are works in progress, and God is doing the work. They are increasingly demonstrating what God can do in someone's life. I trust you are up for an amazing adventure!

FOLLOW-THROUGH 2:
A QUALITY MAN

I have never met a dude who didn't want to be a quality man at some level. But for some reason, most every man, in the pressure of the moment, caves to behavior he despises. Why do so many men desperately want to build a loving, loyal, God-fearing family but watch in horror as their choices work contrary to the very things they say matter most? Too often men tear down with their own hands the good that they set out to build. We easily recognize the phrase "his own worst enemy," because it applies to men with staggering frequency. What is wrong with us? Why do the biblical words, "For I do not do what I want, but I do the very thing I hate" (Rom. 7:15b) resonate so strongly with us? The answer is found much deeper than just our behavior. The problem is in our very nature, and only Christ can free us. As men, we are broken and don't work right; we have fallen and can't get up. Like a mag wheel on a low-profile sports car that's been bent rolling over a curb at high speed, the fix is possible but not easy.

> **How do you relate personally to this picture of bentness? In what areas of your life have you found yourself doing exactly what Paul described in the verse above—failing to do what you know you ought and doing what you shouldn't? Explain.**

Welcome to the history of men. You're part of it. Here's how the damage was done. Adam, the first man, was declared by God to be "very good" (Gen. 1:31) just after the Creator breathed life into him. But Adam's intentional rebellion in the garden propelled him and the whole human race into what theologians call depravity (Gen. 3:17; Rom. 5:12-14). Depravity is the essence of our fallen nature and the state we remain in apart from an intervention by Christ. Depravity means we are unable to choose the right, and we live with a constant inclination toward selfish sin. Like a cowlick that sticks up no matter how many times you slick it back, our nature as men is boldly bent toward badness. Two powerful, sinful tendencies lie at the root of our bad bent. We must conquer them in Christ if we are to become quality men.

The two tendencies I'm referring to are fear and anger. Angry men and fearful men are not quality men. We all struggle with one or both of these tendencies.

> **Stop for a moment, and reflect on the reality of anger and fear in your life. How are these characteristics negatively displayed in your words and actions? To what degree can you admit to yourself that these two tendencies govern a lot of your decision-making?**

Acting like a man means getting victory over fear and anger. Both tendencies motivate us to self-protect, to insulate ourselves from hurt. With fear, we pull back. We fall into passive behavior. But with anger we strike out. We act with aggression. In both instances the path to victory is found in the power of Christ in us to courageously choose faith over fear, compassion over anger, and forgiveness over hurt. How much good is left undone by failing to act like a quality man and conquer your fears? How much damage is suffered by those you love when you fail to act like a quality man and conquer your anger?

> **Take a moment to be quiet before God. Ask Him to help you clearly see how much you allow anger and fear to control your life. In the space below, write what God brings to mind.**

> **Now thank Him for His presence in your life that empowers you to live differently. Ask Him to help you continually take steps to let Him, rather than your anger or fear, guide your life.**

FOLLOW-THROUGH 3:
MAN UP

Doing reps of physical activities, such as practicing a golf swing over and over or shooting lots of free throws, builds muscle memory. Such practice will allow you to perform an action well in a match or game because you have done it so many times before in practice. Similarly, memorizing and meditating on Scripture prepares you to recall and apply the Word of God in critical situations. You will have considered the Word carefully and filled yourself with God's instructions. The Holy Spirit will then use that Scripture to guide, comfort, and correct you and to help you pro-claim the gospel. That's why it's crucial to commit the key verses in this study to memory: "Be watchful, stand firm in the faith, act like men, be strong. Let all that you do be done in love" (1 Cor. 16:13-14). Five short, pointed, clear commands—just like we need them: precise and memorable. There's an edge to this checklist. Its direct wording doesn't give us room for excuses or dodges.

Mark your place, then close this field manual for a moment. Try to say the memory verses out loud. Better yet, find someone to say them to. If you're alone, call up a friend. If you're doing this lesson in a public place, turn to someone nearby (maybe even a stranger) and ask that person if he or she would be willing to listen to you recite some Bible verses you're trying to memorize. Who knows what conversation might come from that exercise?

At the heart of these commands is the phrase we're focusing on this week: "Act like men." Or, as some might say, "Man up!" The phrase doesn't mean we should act in the Hollywood sense of the word. God doesn't want actors. God doesn't want posers or imposters. In this passage, the word *act* means *to conduct yourself*. You are to conduct yourself as a man in the way God defines manhood, not the way the world defines it. This truth needs to be heard in our day when men are so ridiculed and vilified. God needs godly, strong, courageous men.

The Lord said in the Book of Ezekiel, "And I sought for a man among them who should build up the wall ... " (Ezek. 22:30). When God wants something done, He gets a man. Or He gets a group of men. I'm challenging you to be the man God uses to get things done. So, act like a man!

What opportunities do you have right now in your marriage, your family, or your church to step up and act like a man?

If you can't think of any current opportunities for service, who could you talk to about what might be needed from you as a man of God in each of those categories?

One of the crucial lessons I've discovered in the decades I've been a pastor is that men need opportunities to connect and talk with one another. They need relationships and an environment in which they can let their guards down, stop pretending, and be transparent. Men are not failing for lack of content; men are struggling because they lack connectedness, accountability, and meaningful, mutual, motivational community relationships with other brothers in the Lord. It says in James 5:16a, "Confess your sins to one another and pray for one another, that you may be healed." I want to encourage you to stir up a heart of compassion for the other men in your group.

Now, considering James 5:16, anyone who knows the Gospels knows that only God can forgive sins. However, the reason we confess our sins into one another's ears is not because we think that we can forgive one another's sins. We confess our sins to one another to promote vulnerability, accountability, and assurance of forgiveness. Many men (including this writer, at times) wallow in shame and defeat because of a variety of things. So, we keep sin a secret. We hide in our shame. We isolate ourselves. But confessing our sins to one another helps pull us out of that hole. In honesty's light we're able to see that we all fail; we all struggle; we all need Christ. And we're better able to see the need to pray for one another so that we can be healed, changed, and free.

Here's what we know. When it comes to being vulnerable, men (*that would be you*) are more likely to open up with:

1. Assurance of *confidentiality*. If you can't hold in confidence what you hear from other men during this study, you may need to reconsider your participation.

2. Assurance of *mutuality*. As men begin to share, you need to say, "Dude, you can trust us with this. I know where you are." They need assurance of confidentiality and reciprocation. When a guy in your group confesses, "You can't believe what I'm struggling with." Don't respond, "Wow! I just have no idea what you're talking about. You're weird, man! We're going to have to get you into another group." There will be men in the group who desperately need—perhaps more so than you—to confidentially unburden their hearts and be assured of God's forgiveness. You can do that for them while they do the same for you.

    If you were assured of confidentiality and mutuality in your group, what would you need to discuss with other men?

    Pray for each of the guys in your group as you anticipate your next session together.

For more on **Act Like Men**, read *Act Like Men*, Section 1, pages 23-71.

NOTES

BE WATCHFUL

COMPLETE THE VIEWER GUIDE BELOW AS YOU WATCH TEACHING SESSION 2.

The godly man, the biblical man, is a man who is paying _____.

Too many men are _____ and _____.

Men are to be watching for their _____.

Men are to be watching their _____.

It all starts with watching _____.

You can't teach what you don't _____. You can't lead where you don't _____.

The guy you're in charge of is _____.

DISCUSS

DISCUSS THE VIDEO TEACHING WITH YOUR GROUP.

1. What spoke to you or impressed you as you thought about the theme of Session 1, *Act Like Men*? What did you learn this past week through the follow-through days of personal study?

2. Of the five commands in 1 Corinthians 16:13-14, this week we're focusing on *be watchful*. Pastor James emphasized the need for urgency in carrying out our role as men. How do watchfulness and urgency go together?

3. Pastor James made the point that we fiddle, fixate, and philosophize our way into real trouble because those things detract from our watchfulness. How have you found this to be true in your own experience?

4. Why are questions like, "Am I happy?" and "Do I like my life?" irrelevant to a man's job of being watchful?

5. What's the difference between wisely watching over your household and angrily controlling your household? How can you lovingly and effectively track what's happening under your roof?

6. When it comes to finances, every dollar of income gets assigned to one of five uses: spend, debt, save, give, taxes. Name some practical steps a man can take to increase his watchfulness over his family's finances.

7. In the process of watching yourself, name one question you ought to ask yourself each day.

8. How can we pray for you this week as you step up to greater watchfulness as a man?

_____

_____

_____

_____

_____

_____

_____

_____

_____

_____

_____

_____

_____

_____

_____

_____

_____

_____

_____

_____

_____

WEEK 2

PERSONAL BIBLE STUDY

People in ancient cities built towering walls. But they knew that the presence of those carefully stacked stones alone couldn't keep out a determined enemy. The walls had to be manned. Watchmen were stationed at critical places, ready and alert to warn the city of any threat. God's people also knew that even the best watchmen weren't enough. One of the few psalms that was written by Solomon says, "Unless the LORD builds the house, those who build it labor in vain. Unless the LORD watches over the city, the watchman stays awake in vain" (Ps. 127:1).

Just as each of the other manly character traits in 1 Corinthians 16:13-14 is a clear responsibility, *be watchful* is a responsibility that must be accepted with humility. It can't be done alone. You can't build a tall enough wall of rules, install enough extra locks on the doors, or stock your basement with enough guns and ammo to prevent the real enemy from invading. We, as God's men, count on Him to build our houses and watch over our cities. Our prayer is, "God help me, I'll be watchful."

FOLLOW-THROUGH 1:
THE WATCHMAN'S JOB

The word of the LORD came to me: "Son of man, speak to your people and say to them, If I bring the sword upon a land, and the people of the land take a man from among them, and make him their <u>watchman</u>, and if he sees the sword coming upon the land and blows the trumpet and warns the people, then if anyone who hears the sound of the trumpet does not take warning, and the sword comes and takes him away, his blood shall be upon his own head. He heard the sound of the trumpet and did not take warning; his blood shall be upon himself. But if he had taken warning, he would have saved his life. But if the <u>watchman</u> sees the sword coming and does not blow the trumpet, so that the people are not warned, and the sword comes and takes any one of them, that person is taken away in his iniquity, but his blood I will require at the <u>watchman's</u> hand."

EZEKIEL 33:1-6

I've underlined the key word in the preceding Bible passage. If your job is to watch and you don't watch, God Himself will hold you accountable for what goes down because you were asleep at the wheel. God's men should be committed to watching. *Watching*, biblically speaking, represents the idea of *attentive, energetic, focused activity*. (I encourage you to do some personal study on watchmen in the Old Testament.) Watching isn't just passive commentary on a situation. It's observation for the purpose of engagement.

The meaning is clear in the Ezekiel passage. Not only was the watchman supposed to see the sword coming, he was supposed to blow the trumpet and sound the alarm.

> **Name a few people, particularly men, who have sounded the alarm in your life. Whose counsel and cautions in your younger years have proven to be invaluable in the years since?**

Can you remember a time (or several times) when someone from your past gave you advice that you chose to ignore, and you now realize his or her words were exactly what you needed to hear? Explain.

First Corinthians 14:8 says, "If the bugle gives an indistinct sound, who will get ready for battle?" One of the things we continually emphasize at our church that I encourage you to adopt and seek to emulate is a passion for clarity. We always say, "Sometimes people leave church upset, but nobody ever leaves saying, 'What was he trying to say?'" In other words, you might not agree with everything you hear, but you know exactly what it was about. We focus on clarity because we believe that it is a big part of urgency. Your kids may not believe or follow everything you say, but they should be clear about what you are saying. Clarity is a vital characteristic of warning. When the smoke alarm goes off in my house, I'm not trying to figure out what the noise is. I know what the noise is. Effective warnings are always very clear so as to get our attention and let us know what's happening. An effective watchman performs the same function in his home—he sees danger and alerts the people he loves.

Consider the most significant relationships in your life. Have you noticed any red flags or matters of concern in those relationships or the lives of your loved ones that have prompted you to consider warning them in some way? If so, what prevents you from alerting your friends and family?

The initial chapters of 1 Samuel give us the background of Samuel's life. Eli the priest, one of the key figures in these passages, was God's appointed watchman for that time. However, Eli failed in many ways in his life and the lives of his kids. When I think of Eli, I picture the cartoon character Homer Simpson. We know that Eli was obese and that he was a pathetic father.

"Now the sons of Eli were worthless men. They did not know the LORD."
1 SAMUEL 2:12

I know many parents who love the Lord, but their kids don't follow Him. And parents cannot take all the blame for the rebellion of their children. But as I've said many times: You can't do anything to guarantee your kids will follow the Lord, but you can do a lot of things to guarantee that they won't.

Notice what God said of Eli in 1 Samuel 3:13: "And I declare to him [Eli] that I am about to punish his house forever, for the iniquity that he knew, because his sons were blaspheming God, and he did not restrain them." The responsibility was on Eli. He watched while his sons disrespected God, and he did nothing about it. Men, don't let that be your story. You've got to do a better job of watching. Don't settle for passive observation.

When our kids are young, we sometimes have to physically restrain them to keep them from hurting themselves or from disobeying. What forms of restraint do you need to presently exercise with your kids to give them guidance and help them understand you are serious about the role of being a watchman in your family?

How has God been involved in restraining you throughout your life?

In the next two follow-throughs, we're going to look at several specific examples of the type of active watching we need to practice.

FOLLOW-THROUGH 2:
WHAT TO WATCH FOR (PART 1)

The first kind of active watching we need to do is to watch for opportunities to be used by God. It doesn't matter where you work. It doesn't matter how long you've been following Christ. God wants to use your life. He wants to use you in the location where He has placed you. He wants to use you in the lives of people you encounter every day. God wants to use you.

Men who are praying for opportunities, seeking out opportunities, and watching *(Remember, that's what men do—they watch.)* for opportunities to be used by God are going to be utilized in His kingdom. That's the kind of heart we're supposed to have—one that wants to be used.

In the movie *Hoosiers*, Gene Hackman plays a tough basketball coach hired by Hickory High, a small Indiana school, to coach their team. Early in the season, still trying to get his team to follow his coaching, he gives them this ultimatum after a losing effort: "I'm only going to say this one time. All of you have the weekend to think about whether or not you want to be on this team or not, under the following condition: What I say, when it comes to this basketball team, is the law! Absolutely and without discussion!" One guy quits, but his dad makes him come back later. It doesn't take long before they've learned to trust the coach, and they're winning, winning, winning!

Hickory High School, led by its star Jimmy Chitwood, makes it to the state championship and plays a team from a much larger school in a true David versus Goliath clash. In the final scene of the movie, Hickory calls a time-out with the game tied and just a few seconds left on the clock. The coach calls the final play. It's a great movie moment that makes a point I want you to hear.

The coach says, "Listen up! Listen up! Here's what we're going to do! Jimmy, they're going to be expecting you to take the last shot. We're going to use you as a decoy. Buddy, you get the ball, give it to Merle on the picket fence. He's gonna take the last shot. All right, let's go."

The team doesn't move. They just look around at each other. The coach doesn't understand.

"What's the matter with you guys? What's the matter with you?"

Then Jimmy speaks up, "I'll make it."

"Alright," coach responds after a thoughtful moment. "Buddy, get the ball to Jimmy at the top of the key. ... Let's go!"[2]

It's an amazing story with many valuable lessons, but the main thing I want you to see is that Jimmy steps up in the moment. I love that guy! Under pressure he says, "I'll make it." And in the end, he does.

God's men want the ball. I'm not upset if someone who's struggling with an issue approaches me at work needing to talk. I'm not upset if I work with a guy who's a little hard to love. That's what my life is about. I want to be used by God. Instead, I'm like, "Give me the ball. Just give me a chance." That's a big part of being a watchman.

Life is ticking by. None of us are as young as we used to be. For those who are just starting out on this manhood journey, hear this: Life goes by fast. You only get so many sunrises. You only get so many chances to be used by God. There are only so many people right in front of you that you can reach. Now, you want the ball! You want that. Men look for, long for, and watch for their opportunities to be used by God.

> **In what ways are you "asking God for the ball"? In which specific areas of your life are you trusting God to give you the opportunity to take your best shot?**

The second kind of active watching we need to do is watching to protect. Men are to be protectors. First, let me talk to husbands for a moment. You are to protect your marriage. Memorize and meditate on 1 Peter 3:7, "Likewise, husbands, live with your wives in an understanding way, showing honor to the woman as the weaker vessel, since they are heirs with you of the grace of life, so that your prayers may not be hindered."

Here's an eye-opening project. Write out 1 Peter 3:7 as a vertical list of words. Beside each word, reflect on what it means in your marriage. Start with "Likewise." The previous six verses in the passage have a lot to say to your wife; that's her project. You've got to match her intensity and take care of your side of this relationship. Then move to the word "husbands," and think about what it means to be her husband. Now, you take it from there:

- **Likewise:**
- **Husbands:**
- **Live:**
- **With:**
- **Your:**

If you're not married, what are some ways you can serve as a protector for the women in your life?

God's men are on watch. Watching to make sure nothing trips them up. Watching to make sure nothing destroys them or their families.

I'm going to say this as clearly as I know how to say it. If you have the privilege of being married—and it is a privilege—you will need to keep watch over your sexual relationship in your marriage. It's very possible that there will be times when you and your wife will have a different view of your sexual life together. If you are not able to have clear communication about sexual needs, then that could become a conflict filled with anger and resentment. Sex is a gift from God that should bring mutual pleasure for both of you. Get on the same page with your wife concerning this issue. Don't let this become a source of contention between you. And definitely don't seek inappropriate ways to fulfill your sexual needs. Work this out together. That's watching your marriage. That's a decision to protect your marriage.

And note, if there is conflict in the sexual part of your relationship, that usually means you have some other unresolved relational issue in your marriage. You're going to need to resolve this underlying issue before your sexual intimacy is fulfilling for both of you. I don't know how to say it more clearly than that.

Watch for your kids. That's part of your protecting. I have three children, ages twenty-six, twenty-nine, and almost thirty-one, but I'm still watching. Granted, I'm watching in a very different way than I did when they were younger—but I am on it all of the time. I'm talking to every one of them every week: "How are you doing?" "What are you dealing with?" "How's it going?" This never ends. So, whether you have babies, elementary school kids, middle schoolers, college-aged children, or adult kids that are married—whatever you have—this job never ends. Be watching to protect your family.

You might counter with: "Well, they have their own families now. And they're responsible for their families." Right!

But you're responsible to help them fulfill their responsibilities—to encourage, to advise, to hold them accountable. So, be on watch and pay attention.

We're also to be concerned about keeping watch when it comes to one another's families. You may have a brother you need to encourage and challenge about his marriage, how much he's working, or other issues. Do so, but make sure you speak the truth in love from a place of trust. We as men all need that. We're supposed to be watching out for each other. This is a big part of what God's men do.

Think through the list of men in your small group, praying specifically for each of them. If you find you have no idea what some of them might be facing, make it a point to pull them aside the next time you're together and say, "I was trying to pray for you this week, but I struggled to know what you might need. How can I pray specifically for you?"

FOLLOW-THROUGH 3:
WHAT TO WATCH FOR (PART 2)

We not only watch for places to take action and to protect, we also watch to warn. We need to speak up: "If you keep doing X, you're going to get Y." A big part of biblical ministry for God's men, whether leading your family, your marriage, or your small group, is warning.

Galatians 6:7 warns us, "Do not be deceived: God cannot be mocked. A man reaps what he sows" (NIV). Whatever a man plants, he harvests. You have three choices: You can plant nothing; you can plant noxious weeds; or you can plant good seeds into the life of your family. Only one of those choices is going to yield a good crop. Too many men fail to give their families the leadership God intends for a husband and father to provide because of distraction and passivity. Too many men plant sin-filled seeds in their families through sensuality, workaholism, or other false pursuits. Then they are shocked by the shameful harvest. Heed the warning from Numbers 32:23b, "Be sure your sin will find you out."

Have you received warnings recently that you have treated lightly? Explain. As a watchman who is responsible to God, what do you need to do with what you've been shown?

Are there men in your group that you need to warn because of the choices they're making or the circumstances they are in? What's keeping you from sounding the alarm?

We also watch to win. We're watching for opportunities to win people to Christ.

I had a mind-blowing experience at our church on a recent Sunday after the last worship service. An older gentleman was wheeled up to me in a wheelchair, and the guy pushing him said, "He's ninety-two." Wow! Ninety-two! I feel sure I will have been in a box underground for ten years on my ninety-second birthday. I said to the man in the wheelchair, "Dude! I'd love to live to be ninety-two. What's your name?"

He said, "Darl. D-A-R-L." Awesome. Not hard to spell.

"Darl? That's great. It's nice to meet you, Darl." And then the Lord moved in my heart and prompted me to ask, "Darl, have you committed your life to Jesus Christ?"

He said, "No."

That's a lot of birthdays not to be wise to the ways of salvation, I thought to myself. I said, "Well, let me just ask you a couple of questions. Do you believe that Jesus is God's Son?"

"I do."

"Do you believe that He died to pay the penalty for your sin?"

"That's what people tell me."

"Well, what would keep you from just committing your life to Christ right now?"

"Well, I believe everybody kind of has to get there their own way."

Undeterred, I said, "Hang on, Darl. It says in Acts 4:12, 'And there is salvation in no one else, for there is no other name under heaven given among men by which we must be saved.'" Then I added, "So, do you want to just pray with me right now, Darl, and commit your life to Jesus Christ?"

"No, I don't."

"Darl, you're running out of time! You're going to be in eternity, probably like, in seven more minutes." I was not sure this guy was going to make it to his car. I said, "Darl, when is the next time you're going to be sitting in front of a preacher who wants to lead you to Christ and have your eternity changed?" He just kind of looked down and his friend wheeled him away. As he was leaving, I said, "You don't have much time, Darl!"

We're to be watching for opportunities to win people to Christ. I tried my best with Darl. I obediently shared the gospel. But conversion is the Lord's work, right? If you're paying attention this week, do you think there will be opportunities for you to share the gospel? Truthfully, the answer might be yes or no, but that's not the real issue. The real issue is, will you even be looking for an opportunity to speak to someone about Jesus? Are you on watch?

Watching takes attentive energy. Name two specific areas most in need of your attentive energy this week.

What action will you take? And by when?

For more on **Be Watchful**, read *Act Like Men*, Section 2, pages 73-119.

WEEK 3

STAND
FIRM

COMPLETE THE VIEWER GUIDE BELOW AS YOU WATCH TEACHING SESSION 3.

The word *contend* has to do with _____.

When Jude says, "Contend for the faith," he's not talking about your trust in God (Jude 3). He is talking about the _____ of _____ that makes up Christianity.

"Stand firm in the faith" is talking about the responsibility we have to _____ for the faith.

Like boxers, men of God need to keep their _____ _____.

Standing firm means: To stand together in _____, to insist on the best from one another, to hold up the standard of the _____ of God and the reputation of _____.

DISCUSS

DISCUSS THE VIDEO TEACHING WITH YOUR GROUP.

1. How would you explain the difference between "faith" and "the faith" when it comes to Christianity?

2. As you listened to Pastor James, what were the main things you took away from his reading of Jude 1-16 and his comments?

3. What does it mean to contend for the faith? Name an example of someone doing that. Have you ever had that experience? Explain.

4. Pastor James said, "I don't care what the people say. I just want to know what the Word of God says." How does that differ from how many people live their lives and build their faith?

5. What are possible consequences of someone trying to stand firm who has little knowledge about the faith?

6. Name the primary ways in which you have grown in the faith.

7. How do we make sure that the faith we're standing firm in is the real thing?

8. How are you currently increasing your understanding of the faith?

9. When was the last time you explained what you believe about God to another person? What happened?

10. How does godly standing firm or contending affect the way we treat other people, even those who disagree with us?

11. How does Jude 18-19 describe the current condition of our culture?

12. What specific instructions does Jude give in verses 20-23, and how might we act on each one?

13. How do the words of the doxology in Jude (vv. 24-25) encourage you to stand firm in the faith?

WEEK 3

PERSONAL BIBLE STUDY

As God's men, we know that there are certain actions we need to take at certain times. In his letter to the Ephesians, Paul uses the progression of sit, walk, and stand to describe three crucial aspects of our relationship with God. We reach the point of standing firm in the faith (Eph. 6:10-11) after we have understood what it means to "sit" or be "seated" (Eph. 2:6) and what it means to "walk" (Eph. 4:1).

Basically, Paul spends the first three chapters of Ephesians laying out all the God has done in Christ to place or seat us in a life-changing and destiny-altering relationship with Him. We don't seat ourselves with Christ, God does it for us by grace through faith. "Being seated" means being saved. Paul summarizes the process in the familiar words of Ephesians 2:8-9, "For by grace you have been saved through faith. And this is not your own doing; it is the gift of God, not a result of works, so that no one may boast."

Once we understand that our seated position with God is through Christ, and not by our own efforts, we are ready to do some walking. The Bible frequently uses the idea of striding and taking steps as a picture of living. Paul begins chapter 4 by saying, "I therefore, a prisoner for the Lord, urge you to walk in a manner worthy of the calling to which you have been called." The word *therefore* means Paul is referring to all that he has said up to this point. He follows it with a challenge, basically saying: *If what I've just shown you about being seated with Christ and saved by grace through faith is true, then it's time for you to get serious about living that out!*

But Paul's not done. After we're seated with Christ and walking worthy of the life He has given us, we also have to stand. Or as he puts it, "Put on the whole armor of God, that you may be able to stand against the schemes of the devil ... that you may be able to withstand in the evil day, and having done all, to stand firm. Stand therefore ... " (Eph. 6:11, 13b-14a). *Stand* is not in contrast to *walk*. It actually refers to a military tactic used by the Romans to conquer the world. Their soldiers were trained to take control of the space immediately around them. Their individual fighting skills were honed to guard and defend that space against the enemy and function efficiently as a fighting unit. [3]

In the verses that follow, Paul describes the spiritual armor God has provided to ensure we can *stand*. He is envisioning the intense battles we must be ready to engage in the spiritual realm. Standing firm means remaining and defending our little piece of the battlefield in the name of Christ, our captain.

FOLLOW-THROUGH 1:
WHAT YOU BELIEVE

What you believe is incredibly important. What you believe about Jesus, the Word of God, and the church is foundationally significant. What you believe about sin, repentance, and the judgment has ramifications not only for your own life but for those around you who don't know God. What you believe about wise stewardship of finances will shape your life.

> **Why are these beliefs so important? What difference does it make in your life to believe deeply in certain things?**

> **When it comes to acting like a man, are you finding that some of your beliefs have to be set aside or altered because they undermine or conflict with things that are more important? If so, which ones and why?**

Paul said at the end of his life, "I have fought the good fight, I have finished the race, I have kept the faith" (2 Tim. 4:7). He wasn't talking about having lived his life based on a casual belief system. He was talking about putting his life on the line, ready to live or die for Christ. He stood firm in the faith to the end. And we are to do the same as men of God. We can't let our theology gravitate to our behavior. We are to let sound biblical theology call us again and again out of a life of compromise, and out of selfish, shortsighted, self-serving living. We must let robust biblical theology call us to a life of gratitude for a Savior who loves us and gave Himself for us.

What are the consequences of allowing your theology to gravitate to your behavior?

What does a "life of compromise" and "selfish, shortsighted, and self-serving living" look like? How has this been your experience?

Paul used the ideas of fighting, running, and keeping the faith to describe the post-conversion part of his life. Do these ideas describe the way you are living out your life? Explain.

How would you define "robust biblical theology"? Is that how you would describe your theology? Explain.

When Jude said "earnestly contend for the faith," he was calling men to fight for what is true, to fight for what has been revealed in the Bible (Jude 3, KJV). He wasn't talking about the faith it takes to trust in God for salvation, he was speaking of the body of biblical truth that has been passed down through the centuries. When Paul said he had "kept the faith," what did he mean (2 Tim. 4:7)? First, he meant he had kept the faith personally. He had not failed, faltered, or caved. He believed until the end. Second, he meant he had kept the faith going and passed it on. Generations to come would hear the gospel because of his faithful witness to the faith. Third, and perhaps most importantly, he meant he had kept the faith from being diluted, destroyed, or downgraded in any way. He had protected it. Stood for it. Several of Paul's letters (see Galatians) were almost entirely devoted to combatting theological error and drift that he realized would be deadly to the faith.

How have you been "keeping the faith" in each of these ways?
- **Personally:**

- **For Future Generations:**

- **Preserving Right Theology:**

We need men who understand that in failing to stand for the faith that has been entrusted to us, we are doing grave damage to the next generation of potential Christ-followers. Twice the apostle Paul used the term *guard* to picture how Timothy was to treat the gospel (1 Tim. 6:20; 2 Tim. 1:14).

Once we know what our faith is, we have to stand firm in it. It should never be easy for a man to sit under a ministry that is unbiblical in content or emphasis. It should never be easy for a man to take his family to a church where the glory of Christ, the authority of God's Word, and the power of the Holy Spirit are not consistently front and center. Most of us live on spiritual table scraps as it is in our personal walk with Christ, so the church has to be an earth-shattering, window-rattling, life-altering encounter with the God of the universe. Standing firm in the faith means insisting that your family worship, grow, and fellowship in a strong, spiritually healthy church. You wouldn't take your family to a fast food restaurant every night for dinner. And you wouldn't let your children eat out of the neighbor's dumpster. In the same way, you should never give your life or expose your family to a ministry that isn't foundationally, without apology, committed to the authority of God's Word.

Standing firm in the faith means choosing a church that stands firm in the faith. It means instilling godly convictions in your children. It means standing in the truth until the end. No sitting down. No backing up. Being resolute in your commitment to Christ and the gospel. Stand, man. Stand.

FOLLOW-THROUGH 2:
LET'S BE CLEAR

What a man believes about God is the most important thing about him. If you are struggling to believe, struggling to persevere, struggling to carry the heavy weight that God puts on many men's shoulders, you need strong biblical theology to carry you through. Someone has said that too many times we pray for easier paths when we ought to pray for stronger shoes. And the stronger shoes of the Christian life are built from a robust, biblical theology. Your success in acting like a man will be a product of how well you really know God's Word.

**Read the following Scripture passages: Psalm 119:9-11,89-93,97-105.
How do these passages speak to the necessity of God's Word in your life?**

How committed are you to personal, thoughtful Bible study? What needs to improve or change?

If you were to choose a book of the Bible in which to immerse yourself through repeated reading, study, memorization, and meditation, what book would that be? Why this book?

Standing firm in the faith means holding biblical ground without compromise. It is active standing, fighting off the enemy who wishes to tear down the faith and reduce its influence in your life and the world. This is military language that calls to mind the courageous stands taken by the Texan defenders at the Alamo or the Spartans at Thermopylae. It's about having a band of brothers to stand with you no matter how daunting the opposition. And it's vitally important that we stand together, not alone.

What is this *Act Like Men* study teaching you about your need to rely on other men?

Describe one way in which your understanding of godly manhood has been clarified since starting this study.

We need to realize that it's possible for us to spend time and resources standing for the wrong things. We can bust it to be successful by worldly standards. But we all know too well—victory in this world is hollow. I enjoyed cheering for the Chicago Bulls's six NBA championships. And I went out of my way to be in Philly back in 2010 when the Blackhawks won their first Stanley Cup in nearly fifty years. And I was cheering among the long-suffering Cubs fans when they finally won the World Series after more than a century of trying. However, the joy of any victory is fleeting. It may not even make it to the end of the week. How painful this would be if being a Chicago sports fan was my life, as it is to so many men. It's what they live for, wait for, drink for, even breathe for. It's what they talk about, argue about, and—if you have been in the street or local bar after a game—you know it's what they fight about.

How do you relate to Pastor James's thoughts on passion for the temporary? In what areas of life are you investing too much energy, loyalty, and time in what is secondary?

If you're not sure, ask your wife how she would answer the preceding question for you? (Be ready to take seriously what she tells you.) If you're not married, ask a couple of close friends.

Much of the anger and relational dysfunction men exhibit comes from the overflow of despair they feel when they live for a worldly result, expecting it to bring the fulfillment it seems to promise. But when the result is less than what they desired or the euphoria fades quickly, their hopes are dashed. It's pretty tough to stand on the mountain and find that the victory you longed for and worked hard to attain is far less than you expected.

The world of sports is just one example of men getting the urgency thing right but lacking clarity. Being urgent is good, but we need to be urgent about things that matter and outcomes that will last. Most of what men pursue provides neither. For that reason, the Holy Spirit inspired Paul to include clarity in his call to urgency. First Corinthians 16:13 calls us, yes, to "be watchful," but then quickly adds, "stand firm in the faith." We are not acting like men until our urgency is engaged with full biblical clarity.

Take a few minutes to pray for each of the men in your group by name. Think about their specific challenges, and ask God's Spirit to help them each stand firm.

FOLLOW-THROUGH 3:
FIVE GOSPEL WORDS

Earlier, we looked at aspects of *the faith*, but we didn't completely boil it down. I wanted you to recognize the importance of the Bible as the ultimate guide and explanation of the faith. You needed to begin with the big picture of God's written revelation. Let me be completely clear here: God's Word doesn't change; the message doesn't shift. Scripture doesn't adjust to reflect popular thought in current culture. It is forever truth. It's where we stand firm.

One of the great blessings of twenty-five years of ministry in the same city is my relationship with other area pastors. For more than a decade, I met with a diverse group of the pastors of larger churches throughout Chicagoland. We met quarterly, bridging racial, denominational, economic, and other lines that often separate people. We gathered together around our common love for the gospel and the church of Jesus Christ. The experience was life-changing for me. From that fellowship, I began a friendship with Bill Hybels, a pastor from a very different background who pastored a very different style of church.

I will never forget the day Bill shared with our group about his struggle with how to hold the staff of his large church accountable for the essential elements of the gospel message. He challenged each of us to come up with five words that best summarize the gospel. We were to choose words so essential to the gospel that if one of them were not included, salvation wouldn't be possible. To reduce it any further would be to go beyond the irreducible minimum. If you don't have these five things, you don't have biblical faith.

Take a moment to jot down five or six words that you think are crucial to the gospel faith.

Here is a list of five gospel "gotta haves": God, sin, substitution, belief, and life. We have already touched on them in earlier Bible studies and will continue to return to them often.

GOD is a summary term for the Trinity as revealed in Scripture. The Father, the Son, and the Holy Spirit are one. "And I [Jesus] will ask the Father, and he will give you another Helper, to be with you forever, even the Spirit of truth, whom the world cannot receive, because it neither sees him nor knows him. You know him, for he dwells with you and will be in you" (John 14:16-17).

SIN is our universal condition of separation from God. We're born as sinners, "for all have sinned and fall short of the glory of God" (Rom. 3:23), already candidates for God's eternal judgment.

SUBSTITUTION refers to what God did through Christ and His cross to rescue us from sin. He took our place and our punishment as our perfect substitute. "And you, who were dead in your trespasses and the uncircumcision of your flesh, God made alive together with him, having forgiven us all our trespasses, by canceling the record of debt that stood against us with its legal demands. This he set aside, nailing it to the cross" (Col. 2:13-14).

BELIEF is placing our complete trust in Christ alone for forgiveness and eternal life. "If you confess with your mouth that Jesus is Lord and believe in your heart that God raised him from the dead, you will be saved" (Rom. 10:9). Once we believe, we can stand firm in the faith.

LIFE is the present and future promise God gives to those who place their faith in His Son. "I came that they may have life and have it abundantly" (John 10:10).

> **Write out your own definition next to each of the five words that follow. Getting a clear handle on each of these terms would be a compelling act of standing firm in the faith.**
> - **God:**
>
> - **Sin:**
>
> - **Substitution:**

- **Belief:**

- **Life:**

Standing firm in the faith means you not only develop clarity on these core matters, but you also make sure your family knows what you believe and why you believe it. In the context of Joshua's final words to the people of Israel, he issued a definitive challenge about their devotion to the Lord, while making it clear where he and his family stood: "Now therefore fear the LORD and serve him in sincerity and in faithfulness. Put away the gods that your fathers served beyond the River and in Egypt, and serve the LORD. And if it is evil in your eyes to serve the LORD, choose this day whom you will serve, whether the gods your fathers served in the region beyond the River, or the gods of the Amorites in whose land you dwell. But as for me and my house, we will serve the LORD" (Josh. 24:14-15).

> **Regardless of what is going on in the world, is your choice to stand firm in the faith this clear? Explain.**

> **Read Deuteronomy 6:1-9. In what four settings are you supposed to have conversations in your home about God's Word (v. 7)? Are you having these conversations? Why or why not?**

> **When you leave this earth, what will your children remember about your efforts to keep God always in the forefront of your family's life?**

For more on **Stand Firm**, read *Act Like Men*, Section 3, pages 121-163.

WEEK 4

BE
STRONG

COMPLETE THE VIEWER GUIDE BELOW AS YOU WATCH TEACHING SESSION 4.

The strongest man is the man that God regards as _____.

Masculinity and being strong cannot possibly be about those silly _____ that men make. If you're hiding behind a false notion of masculinity and considering yourself strong, God may consider you _____.

Both Jacob and David knew how to _____.

The Bible says God has more affection for one repentant man than over ninety-nine men who don't think they even need to _____.

_____ is the most awesome grace-inducing, blessing-attracting, favor-building thing that a man can to before his God. God loves it, loves it, loves it, when His men _____.

Repentance: A recognition of _____ followed by heartfelt _____ culminating in a change of _____.

DISCUSS

DISCUSS THE VIDEO TEACHING WITH YOUR GROUP.

1. What characteristics define manhood according to our culture?

2. How many of these characteristics would we consider universal—things all men should be?

3. How many characteristics on our list would fit into the biblical definition of manhood?

4. Based on the video teaching from Pastor James, what is the basic definition of a strong man?

5. Do you agree with this definition? Why or why not?

6. Does your life reflect this definition? Explain. What would it take for your life to match this definition?

7. Pastor James mentioned three men from the Bible: Jacob, Esau, and David. What are your impressions of each of those guys?

8. With which of these three do you most identify, and why?

9. Pastor James said, "Repentance is a recognition of sin for what it is, followed by a heartfelt sorrow, culminating in a change of behavior." Why should this be the regular practice of an authentic, strong man?

10. What was Pastor James getting at when he said, "Repentance is the most awesome grace-inducing, blessing-attracting, favor-building thing that a man can do before his God. God loves it, loves it, loves it, when His men repent!"?

11. How can we pray for you this week regarding this matter of repentance?

WEEK 4

PERSONAL BIBLE STUDY

The New Testament Greek word for true repentance is *metanoia*. It means "a change of mind and purpose and life."[4] All change begins with a change of mind. Notice the focus on the word *mind*. Repentance is not a change of scenery. Repentance is not a new church or new job or a new marriage. Repentance is a change on the *inside*—a change in the way I think about something that results in living a different way.

Let's review the three-part definition Pastor James gave us in the video teaching: *Repentance is a recognition of sin for what it is, followed by a heartfelt sorrow, culminating in a change of behavior.* Repentance is change at every level of your being: your mind, your emotions, and your actions.

Only God can bring you to repentance. Second Timothy 2:25b says, "God may perhaps grant them repentance ... " Repentance is a gift that God gives to a person who wholeheartedly seeks Him. But God doesn't force us to repentance; He leads us there through His grace and kindness (Rom. 2:4).

Repentance is not easy. If it were, everyone would be doing it. That's why it takes a strong man to repent, and it's why genuine repentance makes a man stronger.

FOLLOW-THROUGH 1:
THE INTERNAL EFFECTS OF REPENTANCE

When God gives us a clear view of our sinfulness, we are being led into a two-part crisis of repentance: grief over sin and repulsion over sin. First, grief is recognition, ownership, and deep sorrow over sin. It's what Paul is talking about in 2 Corinthians 7:9b, "For you felt a godly grief" and in verse 10, "godly grief produces a repentance that leads to salvation ... " That word *grief* could also be translated "pained, distressed, or sorrowful."[5]

If you're truly repentant, you're going to feel deep conviction about your sin. You will experience internal hurting and soul anguish. You'll be grieved over the wrong choices you made.

> **When was the last time you were greatly distressed and grief-stricken about sin in your life?**

> **What resulted from that realization of sin?**

> **When we're convicted and grieved over sin, how do we try to invalidate or avoid what God is saying to us?**

In Scripture, some people who had a direct encounter with God felt the full weight of their sin. Job, after he realized the foolishness of his words, said to the Lord, "I despise myself, and repent in dust and ashes" (Job 42:6). After Abraham questioned God's plan to destroy Sodom, he became suddenly aware of his place before the holy God. He exclaimed, "Behold, I have undertaken to speak to the Lord, I who am but dust and ashes" (Gen. 18:27). Isaiah, given a vision of God on His throne, fell on his face and said, "Woe is me ... I am a man of unclean lips ... " (Isa. 6:5). A sense of unworthiness is the immediate result of meeting with God. Even the most righteous among us is not coming close to God's standard of unattainable, infinite holiness.

Standing firm in the faith (last week's lesson) includes the magnificent and overwhelming vision of God that drives us to humility and repentance. How does your view of God affect your pride and self-righteousness?

Following hard on the heels of grief over sin comes repulsion over sin. What was attractive and tempting earlier, now becomes ugly and sickening to us. Paul continues in 2 Corinthians 7:11, "For see what earnestness this godly grief has produced in you ... " The Corinthians had been shocked and saddened by the reality of their sin; now they were sickened by it. The word *earnestness* implies diligence, seriousness, and readiness to make changes.[6]

From observation or personal experience, share some examples of how sin that was once attractive became repulsive.

What had to happen to cause such a significantly altered reaction to those sins?

When I'm truly repentant, I exert serious intent and energy toward putting sin behind me. Repentance brings with it a new urgency about my relationship with God and strong negative feelings toward anything that would injure that relationship. What used to be so attractive now repulses me. I'm indignant about its past hold on me and resolutely determined that it will, from now on, be repulsive in my eyes.

Most of us have a food, a smell, or a taste that can almost instantly make us nauseous. Repentance takes place when we feel that way about our sin. We now gag over what we once thought brought us joy. Our thoughts change to *I don't want to act like that anymore. I don't want to say those things. I'm sickened by that attitude. I'm so weary of my selfish sensitivity, anger, and hurt feelings over every little perceived slight from others. When will I grow up and put that behind me once and for all?* Repentance takes place when whatever private satisfaction a specific sin previously afforded, now makes us want to vomit because we see it for what it really is.

It seems that sins generally fall into three categories: pride, pleasure, and priorities. Think for a few minutes about the sins you struggle with in each of these categories. Ask God to show you the sins you're already developing a repulsion for and the ones that still need the work of repentance.

Be particularly wary about ignoring or justifying things we call "little sins" or "not-that-big-a-deal sins" that are actually small gestures of rebellion against God. Grief and repulsion about personal sin are the first two effects of genuine repentance.

Pray for each of the guys in your group. Ask God to allow this week of reflections to move them to repentance that has a lasting impact and brings about real change.

FOLLOW-THROUGH 2:
THREE OUTWARD EFFECTS OF GENUINE REPENTANCE

When repentance takes place, the internal shift in your heart will prompt significant external actions. Repentance has both an inward and an outward effect. Obviously we see this in the most basic moment of repentance—when we recognize our sinfulness and turn to Christ in faith. This starts our entire life as believers, and it includes both an internal and external aspect of repentance and redemption. Perhaps Romans 10:9-10 describes this transformation the most succinctly: "Because, if you confess with your mouth that Jesus is Lord and believe in your heart that God raised him from the dead, you will be saved. For with the heart one believes and is justified, and with the mouth one confesses and is saved." The inward grief and repulsion of repentance lead to external actions toward others, God, and the future. We experience God's strength when we undertake these actions without delay.

Be strong in pursuing restitution. Repentance will move you to be not only right with God but to be right with people. You will experience an immediate and urgent desire to reconcile with people whom your sin has wounded, and fix the fallout. Restitution is a fruit of repentance.

In the Bible, Zacchaeus is a great example of wholehearted repentance (Luke 19:1-10). When he repented, Zacchaeus's first action was to make things right with those he'd cheated. His confession and commitment sounded something like this: *Man, this money doesn't belong to me. I've got to give it back—and I'll do it with interest. I don't want this at my house.* That's why, when Paul affirmed the Corinthians' repentance, he described their response as "eagerness to clear [themselves]" (2 Cor. 7:11).

Repentance doesn't demand anything, but it moves us to humbly seek forgiveness and reconciliation. So, genuine repentance means you need to have a conversation with the people you've injured such as your spouse, your children, your boss, your neighbors, or your friends. All these people will now be able to gladly report that you have done what you can to restore your relationship with them.

How up-to-date are you in seeking forgiveness and reconciliation with those closest to you?

Often, unresolved family offenses create bitterness, resentment, and a stubborn attitude of *I'll apologize when she apologizes* or *They committed the first offense; they should be the one to make the first move to fix things*. But that's probably not going to happen. Strength is expressed in being the first to move towards peace, even when you may not have started the problem. Ask God to show you if you need to make a first move toward reconciling a family relationship.

The strength expressed in repentance leads not only to reconciliation with others, but also to revival in your relationship with God. As a river rushing down a mountainside, God's mercy will begin to wash over your life. Repentance will bring about an obvious restoration of your relationship with the Lord. Your heart will become very sensitive to sin, and you will experience an increased capacity to rejoice in the blessings of God. You'll hunger more for God's Word and have less cravings for things of the flesh. In 2 Corinthians 7:11, Paul mentions "fear," "longing," and "zeal" as strong traits the believers there are exhibiting after repentance. The fear Paul speaks of is the attitude of heart that reveres God and seeks a right relationship with Him. *Longing* is an increased desire to seek first the kingdom of God and His righteousness in all circumstances, and *zeal* is a deeper and clearer passion for holy living.

How do each of these words characterize aspects of your relationship with God?
- **Fear:**

- **Longing:**

- **Zeal:**

If we go back to our key passage in 1 Corinthians 16:13-14, we can see how strength expressed in repentance has a compelling connection to the first three commands in the passage: "be watchful, stand firm in the faith, act like men."

Describe the connection between "be strong" and the commands to "be watchful," "stand firm in the faith," and "act like men."

Genuine repentance also affects our view of the future, pushing us to move forward and not look back. So many of us are submerged in a sea of regrets. One mark of people who haven't repented is that they live their lives in the past. They're stuck. Every day is plagued by reviewing a series of tragic circumstances that lock their focus on what has already taken place.

But notice how Paul highlights the forward-looking aspects of the Corinthians' repentance: "Godly grief produces a repentance that leads to salvation without regret" (2 Cor. 7:10). When repentance is genuine, the heart experiences cleansing from sin, restoration with God, and, by His grace, moves beyond continually beating yourself up for what you did in the past. You know repentance is truly happening in your heart when you get locked in on what's ahead and experience freedom from what's behind.

That's why Paul said to the Corinthians in the previous verse, "So that you suffered no loss through us" (2 Cor. 7:9). Repentance never takes you to a bad place. Repentance is never a waste of time. It is never a shortfall or write-off. It's not a ceaseless cycle of worldly regret. Paul was saying that repentance was not a loss to them but actually a gain because it did its work. It got them out of the rut of a self-condemning past and moved them forward into the freshness of a revived relationship with God. *Today is the first day of the rest of my life; I can't wait for what God has for me next.* When you can say that and mean it from your heart, that's fruit of repentance.

What is your outlook on the future? If you find it riddled with doubts, regrets, and fears, perhaps that's a clue you need to repent. Ask God to help you deal with the past through repentance, so that you can move forward with Him.

FOLLOW-THROUGH 3:
UNDERSTANDING REAL STRENGTH

The video teaching for this session began with the question "What makes a man strong?" You may still be struggling with the answer. We all do. And maybe it wasn't easy to relate to the men from the Bible who were used as examples. But we shouldn't expect to master the countercultural aspects of 1 Corinthians 16:13-14 in a week or even over the six weeks of this study. It will take the rest of your life to put off and learn to resist all the cultural and sinful definitions of manhood and to put on and live God's plan for manhood. It will take strength.

From moving furniture to working on muscle cars, from driving fence posts to carrying groceries in from the garage, men love physical strength and are frequently called to exhibit it. Perhaps when you read our theme verses in 1 Corinthians 16:13-14 and assessed the five imperatives of biblical masculinity, you were most comfortable with the call to strength. Almost every day we get called on to do manly things that require physical strength. It's not a big deal, but it's real.

Stop for a minute and consider the last couple of days. How many "manly things" can you recall doing or being asked to do?

In the opening session we defined acting like men as not acting like a woman, a boy, an animal, or a superhero. How have you been practicing the basic acts of manhood in your setting?

We need to understand that Paul's exhortation for men to "be strong" has little if anything to do with physical strength. In the language of the Bible, the word translated "be strong" is a present imperative verb in the passive voice.[7] This verb form gives two important clues as to its meaning. First, because it is in the present tense, the word connotes continuous action—*be strong now and continue to be strong*. This is not a command for a momentary muscular action. God calls us to have strength in our character and conduct, not simply a stiff upper lip in sorrow or a stubborn persistence during hardship. Strength of godly character needs to be a consistent pattern rather than an occasional response. We tend to be experts at remembering and highlighting that one time three weeks ago when we were thoughtful, while minimizing our consistent thoughtlessness. We can quickly remember that one time we took care of all the household chores when she was sick, but forget how often we shirk family responsibilities to indulge our hobbies.

Here's a little project. Text your wife right now, and tell her you're learning about the importance of being more consistent in your roles as husband and father. Admit you've got a long way to go, but ask her to help you by suggesting three ways you could be more positively consistent in your roles. Yes, that might be a scary thing to do, and it will take some strength to do it, but there's probably no other person in your life better equipped to help you see ways to improve your consistency.

If you're not married, ask a couple of close friends to tell you if they see the strength of godly character in your life on a consistent basis. Ask them to pray for you to be the strong man God is calling you to be.

Because the Greek word for "be strong" is in the passive voice, it indicates that God provides the strength He demands. The strength does not come from inside us but from the Lord. This truth is consistent with other biblical directives about the source of our strength, such as the following: "Be strong in the Lord and in the strength of his might" (Eph. 6:10), and "Be strong in the grace that is in Christ Jesus" (2 Tim. 2:1, NKJV).

In what ways do you derive strength from the Lord? Or to put it another way, describe your practice of dependence on God as you go about your daily routine. Give at least three examples.

Note how Jesus Himself highlighted strength when He was asked about the most important rule to live by. He simply quoted what His Father had stated in the Old Testament: "The most important is, 'Hear, O Israel: The Lord our God, the Lord is one. And you shall love the Lord your God with all your heart and with all your soul and with all your mind and *with all your strength*.' The second is this: 'You shall love your neighbor as yourself.' There is no other commandment greater than these" (Mark 12:29-31, *emphasis mine*). That phrase "with all your strength" doesn't assume that we have an impressive amount of power to bring to our love for God, but it emphasizes that we had better be all in. Truly loving God involves never forgetting that He loved us first and loves us always. Our love is always responsive and never given to generate love from Him. It also involves counting on Him to supply whatever strength we need to carry out what He has planned for us each day. What God said to Paul, He says to each one of us, "My grace is sufficient for you, for my power is made perfect in weakness" (2 Cor. 12:9). We are never stronger than when we are fully relying on God to work in and through us.

As you end this week of focused attention on what it means to "be strong," write out a plan of action for being the strong man God wants you to be. Use your plan to hold yourself accountable and track the progress you are making in the *Act Like Men* components. Expand on the sentence below.

As I understand being strong in Christ, I will pursue the following actions and attitudes, continuing to depend on Him throughout my life:

For more on **Be Strong**, read *Act Like Men*, Section 4, pages 165-212.

LET ALL YOU DO BE DONE IN LOVE

COMPLETE THE VIEWER GUIDE BELOW AS YOU WATCH TEACHING SESSION 5.

On the majors, we are called to _____.

Most things are not _____.

On the minors (and most things are minors), _____.

If winning at home means winning every preference issue, you're not a
_____ person. You don't want to fail at hitting the bull's eye of following
Jesus, which is _____.

Love means you _____ me.

I _____ you when you're more successful than me, but I also
_____ you when you're less successful than me.

In all things _____.

You are not God's man, and you're not acting like a man, if everyone who knows you
isn't saying, "He is _____ in love."

DISCUSS

DISCUSS THE VIDEO TEACHING WITH YOUR GROUP.

1. Let's expand Pastor James's examples of minors that require acceptance from us. What are some other things besides K-cup locations and music volume that fit the preference category?

2. Name some other minors we are tempted to blow up into majors.

3. How have you learned to accept certain things through realizing other things are more important? Give some examples.

4. How do we determine what is a major?

5. What are some majors you're dealing with in your life? What actions are you taking to deal with these situations? What actions do you need to take?

6. When have you witnessed the power of patience in the practice of love?

7. When have you experienced the effects of kindness in the practice of love?

8. How have you seen jealousy and envy destroy a relationship? How can you guard against this?

9. How have you seen love being expressed in healthy and helpful ways among men?

10. What are some ways in which we could more consistently do all things in love in our homes? In our small group? In our church?

11. How can the rest of us pray for you this week?

WEEK 5

PERSONAL BIBLE STUDY

Paul was not exploring new ground with his exhortation in 1 Corinthians 16:13-14. He wasn't creating a new list of the most important parts of life. He was echoing what all of Scripture teaches, including the teachings of the Lord Jesus Himself. When Jesus was asked to summarize what God really expects from us, He basically said, *Love God with everything you've got, and love your neighbor as yourself* (Mark 12:28-34). During the last supper, Jesus showed love to His disciples by washing their feet, preparing to demonstrate the full extent of His love by going to the cross (John 13:1-11). And He said in no uncertain terms, "A new commandment I give to you, that you love one another: just as I have loved you, you also are to love one another. By this all people will know that you are my disciples, if you have love for one another" (John 13:34-35).

Jesus' phrase "just as I have loved you" sets the standard for how we are to love one another. He wasn't talking about a romantic, easy, simple, or conditional kind of love, but the sacrificial love pictured through Jesus serving, helping, suffering, and eventually dying on the cross. Until we include the reality of cost in our idea of love, we're not really serious about loving someone.

Read John's words below. Then take a few minutes to ponder the implications for your life.

> *We love because he first loved us. If anyone says, "I love God," and hates his brother, he is a liar; for he who does not love his brother whom he has seen cannot love God whom he has not seen. And this commandment we have from him: whoever loves God must also love his brother.*
> **1 JOHN 4:19-21**

"Let all that you do be done in love" hits me like a bolt of lighting after the four thunder booms of the other phrases in 1 Corinthians 16:13-14. Unless love is affecting and guiding every aspect of our lives, you and I still have more to learn about acting like men. Fortunately we have a patient God who continues to teach and shape us until His work in us is finished.

FOLLOW-THROUGH 1:
MORE ON THE MAJORS

There wasn't a lot said in the video about exactly what the "majors" are, and you may have a hard time coming up with a good list. But I don't want to leave you hanging, because a lot of us have the tendency to think, *if in doubt, make it a major!*

Surprise! I'm not going to give you a list. But I will give you some principles to help you evaluate what needs to be in the major category. And remember, *On the majors, take action!*

A real man gets out of the chair for something that matters. Paul reflects that in his definition of love in 1 Corinthians 13:6, "[Love] does not rejoice at wrongdoing, but rejoices with the truth."

The truth of the matter is that some things call for action. There comes a time when, if change is to occur, sitting by and waiting won't cut it. We're going to have to move.

How would you describe your "action" button? Is it primed and ready or sluggish and slow? How far do things have to go before you take action in a major situation?

Do your actions tend to be motivated by wise, clear reasoning or by unpredictable, volatile emotions such as anger? Why is the first motivation better? When has the second kind of motivation gotten you into trouble? When have you seen the first motivation bring about a healthy solution?

I'm going to give you a recipe for determining action on a major that tears have been shed over. We have men who are quick to take action, but they do damage because they don't know what a major is. On the other hand, we have passive and weak men who don't act or don't know when to act. Their lack of action can also have devastating results.

Consider it a major situation and time to act when it involves sin. But hang on. Remember, we are all sinners. The Bible lets no one off the hook. Romans 3:10 says, "There is none righteous, no, not one" (KJV). Romans 3:23 adds, "For all have sinned ... " And 1 John 1:10 sets the hook with, "If we say we have not sinned, we make him [God] a liar, and his word is not in us." We are all sinners—no question about that.

So not every sin requires immediate action. If it did, we would be exhausted. It's not your job to create a line in the sand or a crisis every time one of your children proves to be human or your wife expresses some weakness. And keep in mind, it's always easier to make a big deal of others' sins while we downplay our own. We need some ways to recognize when sin requires a significant response. Here are three questions to use as guidelines:

- **Is it a critical path sin?** If failure to take action in this situation will result in major fallout, you have to do something. These include things like an error in central doctrine, marital unfaithfulness, a criminal act, or abusive behavior. Don't just collect stories on that situation, bro. Take some action. Not next month. Take some action quickly if it's a critical path. In this situation, consider: Will this circumstance do damage to the whole? If so, you have to do something. One of the hardest decisions a family will ever have to make is when a part is destroying the whole. As kids move through adolescence into adulthood, the biggest question has to become, "What's best for the family?" Those are painful, hard, difficult days. Churches go through a similar painful experience when they have to make a decision about a member who has stepped out of bounds. Because we live in a world that worships individualism, some people have a hard time understanding why you would take action against a part. Here's why: Just as a doctor would cut out a cancer or a nutritionist would cut out something unhealthy in your diet, so a church, a family, or a man in leadership has to consider, "What's best for the whole?"

- **Is it a chronic, problematic sin?** In other words, it might not be a massive situation, but it might be long-standing. It could be a pattern of smaller issues that continue to cause problems. It could be consistent character flaws that have been observed many times. Regardless, if it is chronic, you may need to take action. You may need to have a loving conversation that concludes with a gentle and humble word of instruction, something like this: "Can I ask you a question? Is it possible that you might have a pattern of gossip in your life that is hurting you and others?" Or maybe you observe an ongoing issue that's moving toward crisis. You know it's a situation where you need to speak a word of truth—"You know, brother, that I love you. So it's not easy to say this to you. But I've noticed you're just not home that much. All you talk about is your job. I see the thing that's going on with your son. I mean, my heart's breaking for you. But maybe part of the problem is that you're just not there enough." Loving intervention doesn't have to be sharp or blunt. Love considers the needed approach.

- **Is it a close, proximity sin?** It's major because it's in your face. It's not your neighbor's issue. It's not your in-laws' problem. (I'd leave that alone for a long time.) It's your wife. It's your kids. Proximity has to do with your immediate responsibilities. "Honey, we're not going to buy that. We can't afford it." Or, "Sweetie, Dad just can't support something that's going to hurt you. Do you understand that I love you so much? And I don't want to keep you from learning what God's trying to teach you, but you can't ask me to get behind something that I know is going to hurt you." Perhaps there are some issues in your neighbors' lives and your friends' lives that you can live with because they are away from you. But these same kinds of issues in those closest to you will call for some kind of loving, and perhaps immediate, intervention.

Review those three questions. Note an example for each situation that you have personally experienced or observed. What action was taken regarding each one?
- **Is it a critical path sin?**

Example:

Action:

- **Is it a chronic, problematic sin?**
Example:

Action:

- **Is it a close, proximity sin?**
Example:

Action:

As someone seeking to act like a man, what is your personal challenge in taking action?

How are you seeking God's help in the wise application of taking action?

FOLLOW-THROUGH 2:
HOW BROTHERS LOVE (PART 1)

Notice what the following verses have in common: "Be devoted to one another in brotherly love ... " (Rom. 12:10, NASB), "Now concerning brotherly love you have no need for anyone to write to you ... " (1 Thess. 4:9), says, "Having purified your souls by your obedience to the truth for a sincere brotherly love ... " (1 Pet. 1:22), and "Finally, all of you, have unity of mind, sympathy, brotherly love ... " (1 Pet. 3:8). They are all biblical reminders about the importance of love between brothers. Here's another: "Let brotherly love continue" (Heb. 13:1).

I love the guys in my small group. I'm not going to let some weird homophobic insanity block me from realizing the necessity of brotherly love. I'm convinced that righteous, loving, mutual relationships between men are essential. You might know that my whole doctoral thesis was on increasing the frequency of disclosure of sin among men. To write that thesis I had to dig deeply into men's sin and note how lonely men can be and how often they live lives of isolation, secrecy, and shame. These secrets and hidden pain need to be brought into the open. One of God's provisions for men's struggles is brothers in Christ. You don't lay those issues on your wife, your mom, or your sister. You lay them on your brothers, understand?

Do you have a band of brothers? If so, who are they? If not, why not?

What do you think you miss when you live in isolation? What are some possible consequences of living in isolation?

The key word in Hebrews 13:1, *philadelphia*, is most accurately translated *brotherly love* or a translation I like even better, *Love like brothers love.*[8] There are movies about how sisters love. There are books and websites about how sisters love. Sisters do love; I'm not questioning that. But the Bible says that there's something about the way that brothers love. *Love like brothers.*

My older brother is very, very dear to me. And I have two younger brothers, one of whom had a severe stroke in 2014. It's difficult to converse with him. He spent most of his life on drugs. My youngest brother is ten years younger than me. I love him dearly, but we are in different stages of life. So I can't really use my relationships with my siblings as an example of what I believe Hebrews 13:1 wants us to pursue. I know that my two sons have the kind of brotherly love the writer of Hebrews is talking about. Their shared relationship with Christ as well as serving together in the church has a lot to do with it. They have a brotherly love that is mind-boggling to me. But I do believe that I experience some of those same characteristics of Hebrews 13:1 brotherly love in my relationships with my closest brothers in Christ. Let me share a couple of those characteristics with you.

First, brothers love faithfully. In Philippians 4:3, Paul calls an unnamed friend in the church his "true companion," or literally, his "true yokefellow."[9] A yoke is a device that combines the power of oxen pulling together. A loving brother is a guy who works hard pulling his share alongside someone else. We want to be the guy shouldering part of the load for his friend. We don't do his work for him, but we let him know that we're in this together for the long haul. That's what brothers do. They love faithfully.

> **Do you have faithful brothers shouldering the load alongside you? If so, how important are they to you? If not, why not?**

> **What would it take for you to be a faithful brother to other men?**

Second, brothers love fiercely. Real brothers don't allow others to come between them. They are staunch allies. Attacking one means attacking both.

Do you remember the biggest fight you saw when you were in elementary school? I certainly do. At my school, I remember two brothers, Fred and Curtis. They were only ten months apart in age, and they looked like twins. Curtis was supposed to have been in the sixth grade, but he failed a year, so he was in the same fifth-grade class as Fred.

I'll never forget the day an eighth-grade bully named Bruce started acting like he owned the playground. To demonstrate his power, he made the fateful decision to pick a fight with Fred, who was significantly smaller. I was blessed to be in the life-changing position of seeing Curtis's reaction when he realized Bruce was beating on his brother. He came across the playground like a Tasmanian devil. Then those two fifth graders absolutely shredded that bully. That's what brothers do. They not only love faithfully, but they also love fiercely.

Interestingly, brothers can fight with each other, but nobody else better fight with your brother. We can pick on each other. But don't be messing with one of us and not expect the other to jump in to defend.

Who's a brother that would be willing to fiercely defend you? Who are some brothers you would fiercely defend?

As *Act Like Men* brothers, this love that is both faithful and fierce forms the first circle of our relationship. I don't have ears to hear anyone running down one of my brothers. If my brother needs to hear something, he's going to hear it from me. I know him a lot better than you know him. Me and my other brothers will make sure he gets everything he needs. We don't need you showing up with half the information, running your mouth.

But let me warn you up front, you will endure injustices at times holding the standard of not running your mouth about your brothers. We don't speak against our brothers even if they're talking down about us. The failure of one is not an invitation or reason to retaliate. We don't run our mouths about our brothers.

And if you act like a faithful and fiercely loving brother, you can confidently expect that you'll have brothers that will do the same for you. We'll discuss this more in your next follow-through.

What needs to change in order for you to establish and keep relationships with other men in which you love as brothers love?

FOLLOW-THROUGH 3:
HOW BROTHERS LOVE (PART 2)

In the last follow-through, we looked at how brothers love faithfully and fiercely. Brothers also love discriminately. Every man is not your brother. Don't call some random guy at work, "Hey, bro." Don't take our thing and go share it with just anyone. We became brothers because of what we have in Christ. We have the same Father, the same Lord, the same Holy Spirit inside us. I know it's super cool now for everybody to "brother" and "bro" everybody. But spiritually speaking, everybody's not your brother. Stop saying that to people that aren't interested in authentic brotherhood. The title *brother* is precious, and it should mean something when we use it. When Hebrews 13:1 basically says, *Love like brothers love*, the writer is speaking of the guys who are going to come running when you need them.

Sometime today make it a point to think about the guys who best fit the category of brother in your life. Text, email, or call them with a simple message: *Thanks for being my brother*.

As you think about that group of guys, ask God to help you recognize when one of them is struggling or in need. It could be that something is going on in one of their lives today. Be willing to reach out, step up, and love your brother. If you already know that one or more of your brothers are in need, note their names and jot down what you intend to do to help them. Then do it.

Finally, brothers love sacrificially. To be a brother who loves like that is going to be costly. You're going to have to do some things that are hard. You are going to have to say some things that are difficult to say.

But you have to do and say the hard things because you love them. And you have to be willing to receive the same tough love from your brothers. Sometimes when I'm facing temptation I think about the promises that I've made to my brothers. And when I don't feel strong enough to do what's right, I rally my heart by reminding myself that my brothers are counting on me. And I don't want to fall in a way that might cause our team to lose yards, if you know what I'm saying. Just know that you are stirring your brothers up to love and good works through your sacrificial love for them (Heb. 10:24). And they are doing the same for you.

Proverbs 17:17 states "A friend loves at all times, and a brother is born for adversity." What a blessing it is to have friends who love us deeply, especially those brothers who stand with us in times of trouble.

When my brother is hurting or when my brother is down, I don't have to ask myself if I care or if I'm willing to help. I was born for this! I turn to my struggling friend and tell him "This is why I am on this earth right now—to be here for you! This is what I am all about! It doesn't matter what it costs. It doesn't matter what it's going to take! I am absolutely totally committed to you!"

Now that's powerful, brothers. God, help us to love each other like that. God, help us to live in absolute, total commitment to one another, not just during the good times, but especially during the times of adversity. Living with that kind of love and commitment is going to set us apart in a culture where men and women change marriages like they change their socks. Where some parents walk out on the children they brought into the world. And where people change churches over the smallest of issues.

Aspire to a lifetime of faithfulness in your core relationships. Desire deeply to be able to look back one day and say, "We loved sacrificially. We gave ourselves to each other for a lifetime, and it has been worth it." That's the long target for *acting like men*.

For more on **Let All You Do Be Done in Love**, read *Act Like Men*, Section 5, pages 215-262.

CLOSING CHALLENGE

COMPLETE THE VIEWER GUIDE BELOW AS YOU WATCH TEACHING SESSION 6.

Absolute, Total _commitment_

I want you to know that I am committed to you.

You will never knowingly _suffer_ at my hands.

I will never say anything or do anything knowingly to hurt you, even if you hurt me.

I will always, in every circumstance, seek to help and _support_ you.

If you are down and I can lift you up, I'll do that.

If you need something and I have it, I'll _share_ it with you.

If need be, I'll give it to you.

No matter what I find out about you, no matter what happens in the future—good or bad—my commitment to you will never _change_.

And there is nothing you can do about that.

You don't have to respond to what I'm saying.

I love you.

And that's what it means to be absolutely, totally _committed_ to you.

Satan's first attack is always to get a _wedge_ between men.

Satan's attack: D _isguise_ , D _ivide_ , and D _estroy_ .

DISCUSS

DISCUSS THE VIDEO TEACHING WITH YOUR GROUP.

1. What is your general reaction to the commitment statement?

2. What would be the benefits of making and keeping such a commitment with a group of men?

3. What would be the potential liabilities of keeping such a commitment?

4. How would you go about deciding to make that kind of commitment with some other brothers in Christ?

5. Pastor James named three actions the enemy takes to keep men from depending on one another: disguise, divide, and destroy. Give some examples of each one of these.

6. How do the five core imperatives Paul gave us in 1 Corinthians 16:13-14 speak to the wedges that come between men?

7. What lessons and ideas are you taking away from these *Act Like Men* sessions?

8. In what ways are you acting more like a man since we began this study six weeks ago?

9. If you were going to encourage other men to participate in this study, what would you say to them about its impact on your life?

10. Given where we are as a group right now, what study or conversation would be a good next step for us?

11. How can we be praying for you as we finish this series? What action steps will you be taking, and how can we encourage you as you move forward?

WEEK 6

PERSONAL BIBLE STUDY

Hebrews 10:24-25 is directed to all believers in Jesus, but has particular application to men: "And let us consider how to stir up one another to love and good works, not neglecting to meet together, as is the habit of some ... " In fact, much of the context of this directive echoes the themes we have been tackling in *Act Like Men*. For instance, verse 23 says, "Let us hold fast the confession of our hope without wavering, for he who promised is faithful." What a great way to say, "Stand firm in the faith!" Holding fast and standing firm are parallel ideas about unwavering, unswerving, long-term discipleship. And the phrase "confession of our hope" is a way to describe our faith in Christ. Whether we're thinking about our faith or the hope based on it, we have neither without the faithfulness of God. We define faith as, *believing the Word of God and acting upon it, no matter how I feel, because God promises a good result.*

Verse 24 tells us to "stir up one another" and makes it clear we are not going to be able to do that if we are not meeting together regularly. We don't stir up one another well from a distance. It requires more of an in-your-face experience. Before a big game, the coach may give a rousing pep talk to the entire team, which can be meaningful and motivational. But just before the game starts, usually the whole team huddles close and stirs up one another to play hard.

What are men to do when we get together? Encourage one another! But how?

The answer is found in that phrase, "let us consider how to stir up one another." The New American Standard Bible translates the Greek word for "stir up" as, "stimulate." The NIV says, "spur one another on." I like the King James Version the best. It says we're supposed to "provoke" one another to love and good works. That's what this whole series is about—trying to provoke you into acting like men— pushing you to do all things in love and encouraging you to do the good works of watching, standing firm, and being strong.

FINAL FOLLOW-THROUGH

When the *Act Like Men* events and emphasis started, I had been thinking to myself, *How do we move discipleship of men forward in our church? What's it going to take to get some synergy going, so it doesn't feel like we're pushing the wagon up the hill, hoping we don't slip and have it roll back over us?* A lot of good things and different things were happening. But I kept thinking, *How can we actually challenge men to follow Christ and be accountable to what Hebrews 10:24 says, "And let us consider how to stir up one another to love and good works"?* It was like blowing on a fire that had died down to the coals. I was doing a lot of considering!

Do you know what I mean? You could still get a fire out of those gray coals, but there wasn't any flame at that point, for sure! Our hearts can get like that. We start out red hot and on fire for Christ, but it doesn't take long to burn down to low heat.

Pull out your phone if you have a calendar app, or grab your calendar if you still use a hard copy. Find the date six months from today. On that date, write down a question for yourself: What have I done to act like a man in the last six months?

Now, what are you going to do in the next two weeks to make sure that when you ask yourself that question, there's a lot to think about?

What would it take for men to fan into flame the decision to act like men again? Well, knowing what I do about men and leading men, I knew that men would have to be pushed and stretched. I've been saying for almost thirty years, "It's easier to get men to do a hard thing than it is to get them to do an easy thing." We can get a thousand men to come and pray for an hour at 3:00 a.m., but we can't get six guys to come and clean the carpets at 4:30 on Saturday afternoon. Men don't want to do easy things; men want to do hard things. They want to be stretched. Men want to explore their unexplored capacities. So, what needs to happen in this process of acting like men has got to lean toward the hard rather than the easy. I don't mean complicated; I mean clear, challenging, and difficult.

How do hard things challenge you to step up as a man more than easy things do?

What are some of the hard things you are consistently pursuing right now as a man?

How has *Act Like Men* provoked you to turn away from some go-with-the-flow easy things in order to take seriously what God has in mind for you?

Describe your commitment to help shape and participate in what the men in your small group are planning for the future.

One of the lasting impacts of the *Act Like Men* study ought to be the default scrolling of the phrases in 1 Corinthians 16:13-14 in your mind, much like the headlines scroll through the marquee in Times Square. Can you visualize the phrases? Be Watchful ... Stand Firm in the Faith ... Act Like Men ... Be Strong ... Let All That You Do Be Done in Love. You've got a phrase for each day of the week, reserving the weekend for other instructions from the One who made you, saved you, and longs to see you act like the man He designed you to be.

Where could you post these phrases from 1 Corinthians 16:13-14 so that you would see them regularly and be reminded of their importance in your daily life?

List the names of the men in your small group, and commit to pray for them regularly.

As you pray for them, keep their individual situations in mind as you apply Hebrews 10:24, considering "how to stir up one another to love and good works."

ENDNOTES

WEEK 1

1. Thomas D. Lea and Hayne P. Griffin, Jr., *The New American Commentary – 1, 2 Timothy, Titus, Volume 34* (Nashville: B & H Publishing Group, 1992).

WEEK 2

2. Angelo Pizzo, *Hoosiers*, directed by David Anspaugh (1986; Beverly Hills, California: MGM Home Entertainment, 2012), DVD.

WEEK 3

3. Richard A. Gabriel, *The Ancient World* (Westport, CT: Greenwood Press, 2007), 131.

WEEK 4

4. M.G. Easton, *Illustrated Bible Dictionary* (New York: Cosimo, Inc, 2005) via MyWsb.com, accessed on November 27, 2017.

5. William D. Mounce, *Mounce's Complete Expository Dictionary of Old and New Testament Words* (Grand Rapids, Michigan: Zondervan, 2006) via mywsb.com, accessed on November 28, 2017.

6. "Definition of Earnestness" *Blue Letter Bible* https://www.blueletterbible.org/lang/lexicon/lexicon.cfm?Strongs=G4710&t=ESV, accessed on November 28, 2017.

7. "Definition of Be Strong" *Blue Letter Bible* https://www.blueletterbible.org/lang/lexicon/lexicon.cfm?Strongs=G2901&t=ESV, accessed on November 28, 2017.

8. "Definition of Brotherly Love" *Blue Letter Bible* https://www.blueletterbible.org/lang/lexicon/lexicon.cfm?Strongs=G5360&t=ESV, accessed on November 28, 2017.

9. "Definition of Companion" *Blue Letter Bible* https://www.blueletterbible.org/lang/lexicon/lexicon.cfm?Strongs=G4805&t=ESV, accessed on November 28, 2017.

ANSWER KEY

SESSION 1: INTRO
Burden
Bible verse
Conversation
Vision
Woman
Animal
Boy
Superhero

SESSION 2: WATCH
Attention
Fiddling, Fixating
Families
Finances
Yourself
Know, Go
You

SESSION 3: STAND FIRM
Boxing
Body, Truth
Contend
Guard Up
Love, Word, Christ

SESSION 4: BE STRONG
Strong
Distinctions, Weak
Repent
Repent
Repentance, Repent
Sin, Sorrow, Behavior

SESSION 5: LET ALL YOU DO BE DONE IN LOVE
Action
Majors
Acceptance
Loving, Love
Before
Accept, Accept
Love
Growing

SESSION 6: CLOSING CHALLENGE
Commitment
Suffer
Support
Share
Change
Committed
Wedge
Disguise, Divide, Destroy

ADDITIONAL STUDIES FROM JAMES MACDONALD

THINK DIFFERENTLY: NOTHING IS DIFFERENT UNTIL YOU THINK DIFFERENTLY
10 sessions

Learn to renew your mind in Christ as you identify and overcome the mental, familial, and self-created strongholds that enslave you.

Bible Study Book 005644087 **$12.99**
Leader Kit 005399896 **$99.99**

LifeWay.com/ThinkDifferently

LORD, CHANGE MY ATTITUDE: BEFORE IT'S TOO LATE
10 sessions

Look to the Israelites' journey out of Egypt to identify attitudes that dishonor God, disrupt your relationship with Him, and hinder your spiritual growth.

Bible Study Book 005790073 **$14.99**
Leader Kit 005790074 **$149.99**

LifeWay.com/ChangeMyAttitude

AUTHENTIC: DEVELOPING THE DISCIPLINES OF A SINCERE FAITH
7 sessions

Develop a closer walk with God by practicing the spiritual disciplines Jesus Himself used: Bible study, prayer, fasting, fellowship, service, and worship.

Bible Study Book 005470535 **$11.99**
Leader Kit 005399891 **$99.99**

LifeWay.com/Authentic